The Garden
Planner, Journal And log Book

200 Pages — 8.5 x 11
Copyright 2020 © Sbais Press
All rights reserved

Garden PROBLEMS

YEAR: _____

DATE	PLANT	PROBLEM	SOLUTION

Garden TOOL INFO

TOOL	PURPOSE	MAINTENANCE	DATE PURCHASED	SOURCE	NOTES

Monthly HARVEST CALENDAR

MONTH	MONTH	MONTH
MONTH	MONTH	MONTH
MONTH	MONTH	MONTH

Gardening PROJECTS

YEARLY GOALS

NEW PROJECTS

TECHNIQUES

NOTES

Produce BUDGET

FRUIT/VEGETABLE	WEIGHT/QTY	PRICE	MONTHLY	YEARLY

Planting TRACKER

PLANT	QTY	START	TRANSPLANT	SPACING	HARVEST DATE

Garden WISH LIST

What fruits or vegetables would you like to grow?

Garden BUDGET

YEAR: _____

VEGETABLES	AMOUNT
SUBTOTAL :	

FERTILIZER/ MISC	AMOUNT
SUBTOTAL :	

FRUITS	AMOUNT
SUBTOTAL :	

FLOWERS	AMOUNT
SUBTOTAL :	

FLOWERS	AMOUNT
SUBTOTAL :	

Seedlings

SEASON: _____ YEAR: _____

CROP	VARIETY	START	TRANSPLANT	BED/ROW

Weekly TO DO LIST

Monday

Tuesday

Wednesday

Thursday

Friday

Saturday

Sunday

Notes

Pest Control Record

BED/ROW	CROP/FAMILY	PEST	DISEASE	TREATMENT

Sowing TRACKER

SEASON: _____ YEAR: _____

CROP	VARIETY	SOW/TRANSPLANT	BED/ROW

Seed INVENTORY LOG

YEAR: _____

CROP/VARIETY	SEED COMPANY	PURCHASE DATE	QTE

Garden ORGANIZER

YEAR : _____

BED / ROW	CROPS	SEASON	HARVEST BY	NEXT CROPS

Harvest TRACKER

DATE	CROP	QUANTITY	NOTES

Crop ROTATION LOG

PLANT	FOLLOW WITH	DONT FOLLOW WITH

Seasonal TASKS

Spring

- [ ] _____
- [ ] _____
- [ ] _____
- [ ] _____
- [ ] _____
- [ ] _____
- [ ] _____

Summer

- [ ] _____
- [ ] _____
- [ ] _____
- [ ] _____
- [ ] _____
- [ ] _____
- [ ] _____

Fall

- [ ] _____
- [ ] _____
- [ ] _____
- [ ] _____
- [ ] _____
- [ ] _____
- [ ] _____

Winter

- [ ] _____
- [ ] _____
- [ ] _____
- [ ] _____
- [ ] _____
- [ ] _____
- [ ] _____

Square FOOT GARDEN

SEASON: _____ YEAR: _____

Gardening Notes

Succession PLANTING

YEAR : _____

PLANT	SOWING DATES	SEASON	BED/ROW

Weekly PLANNER

WEEK OF : _____

		Notes
Monday		
Tuesday		
Wednesday		
Thursday		
Friday		
Saturday		
Sunday		

Weekly PLANNER

WEEK OF: _____

	Notes
Monday	
Tuesday	
Wednesday	
Thursday	
Friday	
Saturday	
Sunday	

Weekly PLANNER

WEEK OF : _____

	Notes
Monday	
Tuesday	
Wednesday	
Thursday	
Friday	
Saturday	
Sunday	

Weekly PLANNER

WEEK OF : _____

	Notes
Monday	
Tuesday	
Wednesday	
Thursday	
Friday	
Saturday	
Sunday	

Weekly PLANNER

WEEK OF : _____

	Notes
Monday	
Tuesday	
Wednesday	
Thursday	
Friday	
Saturday	
Sunday	

Weekly PLANNER

WEEK OF : _____

	Notes
Monday	
Tuesday	
Wednesday	
Thursday	
Friday	
Saturday	
Sunday	

Weekly PLANNER

WEEK OF : _____

	Notes
Monday	
Tuesday	
Wednesday	
Thursday	
Friday	
Saturday	
Sunday	

Weekly PLANNER

WEEK OF: _____

		Notes
Monday		
Tuesday		
Wednesday		
Thursday		
Friday		
Saturday		
Sunday		

Weekly PLANNER

WEEK OF : _____

	Notes
Monday	
Tuesday	
Wednesday	
Thursday	
Friday	
Saturday	
Sunday	

Weekly PLANNER

WEEK OF : _____

		Notes
Monday		
Tuesday		
Wednesday		
Thursday		
Friday		
Saturday		
Sunday		

Weekly PLANNER

WEEK OF: _____

	Notes
Monday	
Tuesday	
Wednesday	
Thursday	
Friday	
Saturday	
Sunday	

Weekly PLANNER

WEEK OF : _____

		Notes
Monday		
Tuesday		
Wednesday		
Thursday		
Friday		
Saturday		
Sunday		

Weekly PLANNER

WEEK OF : _____

	Notes
Monday	
Tuesday	
Wednesday	
Thursday	
Friday	
Saturday	
Sunday	

Weekly PLANNER

WEEK OF : _____

		Notes
Monday		
Tuesday		
Wednesday		
Thursday		
Friday		
Saturday		
Sunday		

Weekly PLANNER

WEEK OF : _____

	Notes
Monday	
Tuesday	
Wednesday	
Thursday	
Friday	
Saturday	
Sunday	

Weekly PLANNER

WEEK OF : _____

	Notes
Monday	
Tuesday	
Wednesday	
Thursday	
Friday	
Saturday	
Sunday	

Weekly PLANNER

WEEK OF : _____

	Notes
Monday	
Tuesday	
Wednesday	
Thursday	
Friday	
Saturday	
Sunday	

Weekly PLANNER

WEEK OF : _____

	Notes

Monday	
Tuesday	
Wednesday	
Thursday	
Friday	
Saturday	
Sunday	

Weekly PLANNER

WEEK OF : _____

	Notes
Monday	
Tuesday	
Wednesday	
Thursday	
Friday	
Saturday	
Sunday	

Weekly PLANNER

WEEK OF: _____

		Notes
Monday		
Tuesday		
Wednesday		
Thursday		
Friday		
Saturday		
Sunday		

Weekly PLANNER

WEEK OF : _____

	Notes
Monday	
Tuesday	
Wednesday	
Thursday	
Friday	
Saturday	
Sunday	

Weekly PLANNER

WEEK OF : _____

	Notes

Monday	
Tuesday	
Wednesday	
Thursday	
Friday	
Saturday	
Sunday	

Weekly PLANNER

WEEK OF : _____

	Notes
Monday	
Tuesday	
Wednesday	
Thursday	
Friday	
Saturday	
Sunday	

Weekly PLANNER

WEEK OF: _____

Monday	
Tuesday	
Wednesday	
Thursday	
Friday	
Saturday	
Sunday	

Notes

Gardening Notes

Gardening Notes

Gardening Notes

Gardening Notes

Gardening Notes

Gardening Notes

Gardening Notes

Gardening Notes

Gardening Notes

Gardening Notes

Gardening Notes

Gardening Notes

Gardening Notes

Gardening Notes

Gardening Notes

Gardening Notes

Gardening Notes

Gardening Notes

Gardening Notes

Gardening Notes

Gardening Notes

Gardening Notes

Gardening Notes

Gardening Notes

Gardening Notes

Gardening Notes

Gardening Notes

Gardening Notes

Gardening Notes

Gardening Notes

Gardening Notes

Gardening Notes

Gardening Notes

Gardening Notes

Gardening Notes

Gardening Notes

Gardening Notes

Gardening Notes

Gardening Notes

Gardening Notes

Gardening Notes

Gardening Notes

Gardening Notes

Gardening Notes

Gardening Notes

Gardening Notes

Gardening Notes

Gardening Notes

Gardening Notes

Gardening Notes

Gardening Notes

Gardening Notes

Gardening Notes

Gardening Notes

Gardening Notes

Gardening Notes

Gardening Notes

Gardening Notes

Gardening Notes

Gardening Notes

Gardening Notes

Gardening Notes

Gardening Notes

Gardening Notes

Gardening Notes

Gardening Notes

Gardening Notes

Gardening Notes

Gardening Notes

Gardening Notes

Gardening Notes

Gardening Notes

Gardening Notes

Gardening Notes

Gardening Notes

Gardening Notes

Gardening Notes

Gardening Notes

Gardening Notes

Gardening Notes

Gardening Notes

Gardening Notes

Gardening Notes

Gardening Notes

Gardening Notes

Gardening Notes

Gardening Notes

Gardening Notes

Gardening Notes

Gardening Notes

Gardening Notes

Gardening Notes

Gardening Notes

Gardening Notes

Gardening Notes

Gardening Notes

Gardening Notes

Gardening Notes

Gardening Notes

Gardening Notes

Gardening Notes

Gardening Notes

Gardening Notes

Gardening Notes

Gardening Notes

Gardening Notes

Gardening Notes

Gardening Notes

Gardening Notes

Gardening Notes

Gardening Notes

Gardening Notes

Gardening Notes

Gardening Notes

Gardening Notes

Gardening Notes

Gardening Notes

Gardening Notes

Gardening Notes

Gardening Notes

Gardening Notes

Gardening Notes

Gardening Notes

Gardening Notes

Gardening Notes

Gardening Notes

Gardening Notes

Gardening Notes

Gardening Notes

Gardening Notes

Gardening Notes

Gardening Notes

Gardening Notes

Gardening Notes

Gardening Notes

Gardening Notes

Gardening Notes

Gardening Notes

Gardening Notes

Gardening Notes

Gardening Notes

Gardening Notes

Gardening Notes

Gardening Notes

Gardening Notes

Gardening Notes

Gardening Notes

Gardening Notes

Gardening Notes

Gardening Notes

Gardening Notes

Gardening Notes

Gardening Notes

Gardening Notes

Gardening Notes

Gardening Notes

Printed in Poland
by Amazon Fulfillment
Poland Sp. z o.o., Wrocław